Acknowledgement

The background of the book are not just one but many. To make apps from API are usually not very easy and also not so cost effective. Specially, in the financial sector it is really difficult to make apps to make easy transactions and manage finance in very controlled way. Though, there are some APIs but they are not so much cost effective. At this crisis hour of the financial sectors, a concept came to the author to do some research on how can an API can be free, cost effective and at the same time beneficial to make life easier in the financial sectors.

So the author thought he could try and do some researches on some open source APIs likes of OpenMAMA and SMART API. Basically, Open MAMA is more preferred on this matter than the SMART API. And also that it is very compatible with any system and also the direct approach OpenMAMA is very attractive for any developer. Also, it really helps the system to be very cost effective is also a very important characteristics of OpenMAMA. On the other hand to work with something which is not tried out yet has also come into the author mind.

As a result author has chosen SMART API which is mostly used in health and medical tasks to be in the author research list. And during the research author has found much relevant evidence that SMART API has the potential to be used in the financial sector if fallen into the right hands. These research really motivated author a lot to have a go in this analysis. The analysis also believe if we can really try then the cost of financial sectors and also money transactions process can be really kept under control by the help of these API's. The analysis has given a lot of examples and also give a financial model in these book so it can demonstrate how easy and cost friendly can these open source API's can be. Besides, it was also motivated to think what blessings it can bring to the financial engineering sectors.

Also that the author friends and well wiser did help him with all the things needed to be done like helping him with new concepts, providing him with slides and lectures. They also gave the author some videos as well as some valuable suggestions regarding the book. So, that was the main reason behind writing this book.

The expectation of the author of this book is given below:

"In this book I have discussed about the financial engineering based on APIs system. I have also discussed about financial modeling, Detail information about OpenMAMA and SMART APIs etc. I have tried hard to proof the connections of this two APIs in the financial engineering and financial transaction modeling. Besides I have provided OpenMAMA and SMART APIs features, advantages, disadvantages, their usability and compatibility etc in the financial engineering task. The most important thing of the book is API based financial transaction modeling system development which I have design and discussed in the "3.0 Main body of the analysis" section.

I have written this book in book based book writing process. I don't follow traditional technical book writing process. Because I think book based technical book writing process is helpful for article, analysis & research paper etc writing. And this process makes a book easy to understand to its reader. So by reading my book a reader can easily understand the topics of the book and he/she can easily gather the ideas about how to write academic, non-academic book analysis, research paper, article etc. I hope my book will be helpful for the future research about this API based financial engineering.

So I can say that this book is beneficial for the long run development of API based financial engineering."

Abstract

Financial Engineering is now a versatile word in the banking domain and more programmers are now very attracted to it as it has lot to offer to them. Due to these new API's the financial tasks and economic operations have now become a very trivial process than it used to be. The using of these API has helped a lot in solving many banking problem. The most important aspect of the financial API's are that they are very much compatible and have a simple minded approach as a result financial problems are now no longer a problem and are in full control of human race.

Open Middleware Agnostic Messaging API (OpenMAMA) is one of the open standard API has added new dimension to the computational finance. It gives the flexibilities to its users to make application without higher abstractions. Its adaptive quality is also very much noteworthy as it can fit to the requirement without any damaging change to the source codes. Another, SMART API is also a free and open source platform based web standard which helps in making applications of various ranges.

This book looks through different techniques and researches on how can different applications can be made of financial transactions and using of OpenMAMA in present financial sectors. Besides, it will also put some light on SMART API and its compatibility factor regarding how suitable it is to produce Apps from it in financial engineering. This analysis will also focus on cost handling issue as well and will provide some research on how it is more cost effective being a open source web standard. Finally, this book will also discuss how can this API's help to maintain a low-maintenance in financial sector and how can it enhance the performance in creating financial models and transactions.

Copyright

The copyright of this book is registered. None can publish this book or part of it without the permission of the author. If anyone copy, publish, print and plagiarized the book will be illegal offence in the eye of law and be punished.

Table of Contents

Section-A..6

1.0 Introduction..6

1.1 General Question about API Based Financial Engineering...............................8

1.2 Artefact to be developed..9

1.3 Objectives..9

1.4 Structure of the Analysis...11

Section-B..12

2.0 Literature Review..12

Section-C..18

3.0 Main body of the Analysis..18

3.1 Full Information of the Artefact of API Based Financial Engineering...........18

3.2 Constructive API Based Financial Transaction Modeling..............................19

3.2.1 Case Study of Constructive API Based Financial Transaction Modeling...20

3.3 Recommendations for Constructive API Based Financial Transaction Modeling...........46

3.4 Summary of the Constructive API Based Financial Transaction Modeling Analysis......47

3.5 Answering the General Question..48

3.5.1 The Use of OpenMAMA in the Present Financial Sectors..........................49

3.5.2 Research on Smart API and how can it Help in the Sectors of Financial Engineering.................53

Section-D..57

4.0 Conclusion...57

Section-E..61

5.0 Critical evaluation...61

Section-F..62

References and Bibliography..62

Section-A

1.0 Introduction

Technological innovation has considerably innovative the use of financial instrument over the past few years. In that time, the exercise of "open outcry" transaction has been modified by digital transaction systems for bank, insurance, and Share market, among other places. This move has fundamentally changed the way these marketplaces act and has led to higher trading. (Robert Dubil 2011) defined Financial Engineering encompasses the analysis of the efficiency of financial tasks, business principles and economic operations using engineering approaches, mathematical techniques and computational semantics as well as the optimization of existing scenarios to device new financial products (Reitz and Noël 2006). It involves the use of a combination of technical tools from the fields of mathematics, computer science, statistics and economics by financial engineers, who apply these concepts to business operations.

Therefore, computer programmers and system analyst working in the financial data base management system are called financial engineers. Two significant sub-fields of financial engineering are namely computational finance and mathematical finance. The former entails the descriptions of the data and algorithms utilized in financial modeling while the latter is the theoretical utility of mathematics to economic concepts. There exist a wide application use for financial management such as corporate and non-corporate finance, risk management, financial regulations and trading to mention a few in a broad range of institutions including banks and insurance agencies (Robert Dubil 2011).

The utility of OpenMAMA helps to fill the gap in the increasing volumes of business data by providing users with the flexibility to create applications without concerns about the high-level abstractions. It is an open standard that also eliminate the problem of vendor lock-in by proprietary applications. It allows the customization of applications to fit varying features without colossal changes to source codes and total afford of different application platforms. Employing this technology to business transactions is very much profitable for organization.

The SAMRT API is the new set of API that is invented by SMART organization. From the beginning of SMART API book the inventors thought it would helpful for medical science task and Hospital management but after completing the book they are used this API for financial Engineering task achieve great success in this field. This is much simpler API then OpenMAMA API because OpenMAMA has some critical programming coding which is hard for some financial Engineer to understand these coding. But SMART API coding is very simple and anyone can use it by using some popular programming language like C/C++, python, JAVA script etc. The performance of this API is outstanding in the financial sectors like Share market, payment market, bank, Insurance, leasing company etc.

They are cost-effective, secure the investment, timely marketing of new products and possess wide acceptability. Furthermore, the adoption of messaging API to financial transactions makes the adaptability of users to trends in business innovation easy. The flexibility of these applications due to their non-dependence on the underlying middleware technologies is another important merit. The architecture of OpenMAMA utilizes publish-subscribe mechanism for interpersonal communications. This allows messages to be published to distinct topics, and subscribers are able to express interest in them and receive updates accordingly.

This flexibility and affords provide greater scalability in financial transaction. Predicated on the above, the applicability of OpenMAMA to financial engineering of finance models and the transaction is worthy of note. The OpenMAMA API enables financial engineering developers to define trading strategies without concern for middleware implementations. It further helps in their ability to make effective decisions on trading strategies based on transaction criteria.

1.1 General Question about API Based Financial Engineering

There are some common general questions about API Based Financial Engineering. Most of the financial engineering related persons as well as general persons who have small ideas about APIs, e-commerce, financial engineering, financial transaction modeling etc. also want to know the answer of these questions.

The primary goal is to determine suitable answers about API based financial modeling, which can efficiently show data and algorithms related to financial modeling based on OpenMAMA and SMART APIs. So the analysis therefore, seeks to proffer solutions to the following proposed general questions.

1. Investigate and review financial transaction models using APIs based on OpenMAMA in real-life scenarios.

2. Research the use of OpenMAMA in the present financial sectors.

3. Research on Smart API and how can it help in the sectors of financial engineering.

4. Research the proper use of OpenMAMA in financial modeling.

The writer of the book has done a great job to answering this above questions in the "Answering the General Question" part of the book. We hope you will like that answer.

1.2 Artefact to be developed

The objective includes
- Evaluation of the efficiency of financial transaction models using a case study.
- Making reliable recommendations based on the evaluation process above in order to reconcile academic thinking with industrial ethics.

1.3 Objectives

This book has some important objectives which are given below:
- The capability to calculate, store, process, use and re-use information of all types and from all resources easily and to make it available anywhere from several devices.

- Computerized low-maintenance techniques that allow for easy replication.

- The capability to considerably generate down handling costs.

- New techniques to creating firmly incorporated techniques based on best-of-class components.

- Improved performance and threat analytics.

- Developing financial software by using OpenMAMA API in C/C++ programming language.

- Find the advantages and disadvantages of OpenMAMA API.

- Researching the best features of OpenMAMA API for financial engineering.

- Research on features and advantages of Smart API.

- To analyze how Smart API can help in different sectors of financial engineering.

1.4 Structure of the Analysis

1. Introduction: The Introduction of the analysis is composed of the basic and compact knowledge given on financial engineering along with some information about OpenMAMA and SMART API.

2. Literature Review: It shares some previous concepts researches done by some other researcher. Even some personal opinion and examples were also added in this part. It discusses how relevant the topic of the book is provided with which we are working with. For example: OpenMAMA and SMART API.

3. Main body of the Analysis: This part of the analysis explains and discusses about the artifact in information. It forms the logical and analytical background of the book. This part mainly evaluates how the book is relevant and how the aims and objectives can be reached through the use of the aforementioned API's. Finally, some recommendations are also provided in this part long with the summary of the result obtained during the book.

4. Conclusion: It discusses about the ending of the book.

5. Critical Evaluation: It surveys the analysis every aspects very carefully and observes it's every procedure step by step. It also compares how much fruitful will the book be and finally also includes self evaluation after doing the book.

6. Reference and Bibliography.

Section-B

2.0 Literature Review

Financial engineering is mainly focusing on the financial transaction. The most important task of the financial transaction is to complete the transaction process swiftly and securely. So the financial engineering based transaction has some features. The main features focusing on financial transaction are as follows:
- To complete the financial transaction process swiftly.
- To use some transaction model for nicely complete the transaction process.
- To develop API based transaction model.
- To complete the transaction process in a secure way.
- To save the transaction history and data of its user.
- To use electronic transaction system in financial transaction.

The OpenMAMA application technology is an open-source Application Programming Interface (API), which facilitates the interactions of multiple transports and applications (Taft 2012).OpenMAMA is a top rated, open source Middleware Agnostic Messaging API (MAMA) that provides a typical, consistent interface for moving data between high volumes, low latency messaging programs. Demand for top rated messaging in multiple sectors has led to a variety of products from a variety of providers, often leading to complex incorporation circumstances.

The OpenMAMA book is a collaborative effort to develop a typical, ultra-high-performance middleware API that joins a variety of messaging application, reducing incorporation difficulties and boosting time to implement. OpenMAMA uses a typical publish/subscribe idiom (pub/sub).

In this messaging system the information are not sent straight to the receiver, but released to a subject. Members show attention in one or more subjects, and get only messages that attention them. This decoupling of marketers and subscribers allows for higher scalability.

OpenMAMA was declared few years ago and is a part of A Linux Foundation Lab, which includes other open and collaborative development books that advance A Linux or the A Linux environment. Members in OpenMAMA include Bank of America Merrill Lynch, IBM, EMC, Exegy, Fixnetix, J.P. Morgan and NYSE Technologies, among others.

One-year book milestones for OpenMAMA API include:

Eight software connects have been developed for the book from a variety of companies. Bridges allow application interface programs to pass information through OpenMAMA, removing complexity and work when developing several information resources with several users and reducing the difficulty of assisting customized and complicated environments. Bridges and members include:

- AMQP implementation of Qpid, written and contributed by Red Hat
- Avis, written and contributed by NYSE Technologies
- Bloomberg Open API, written, supported and contributed by Tick 42
- Data Fabric Multi Verb, written and supported by NYSE Technologies
- Exegy, written and supported by Exegy
- LBM, written and supported by NYSE Technologies

- Rai, written and supported by Rai
- WebSphere Front Office, under development by IBM

The OpenMAMA software collection is now completely free, along with a particular API for market data known as OpenMAMDA and language supported for C, C++, Java, and .Net. This finishes the start seeking process started by book members a year ago. From this point of view, all improvements to the OpenMAMA codebase will come from the free book, using open source development methods.

The accessibility to OpenMAMA Enterprise Edition, a commercial supported and qualified submission of OpenMAMA from NYSE Technologies. This new providing is available from NYSE Technologies these days as part of its open platform.

The video presentation of (O' Sullivan 2012) at the collaboration summit organized by the Linux foundation on 3rd April, 2012 highlighted the fundamental motivation for the conception of the OpenMAMA platform based on the need to reduce trading problem. It emphasizes its core functional aspect of the message oriented middleware (MOM) architecture that allows the communications between various applications differing in levels of abstractions without the need for the knowledge of one another.

This flexibility is due to the internal framework of the OpenMAMA operates on two communication concepts; the first is the use of publish-subscribe and queues while the second underlying features operates on topic-based naming for message routing.

Furthermore, the presentation discusses the compatibility of the OpenMAMA architecture with a variety of MOM platforms. Apart from this, the applications of OpenMAMA provide means to surmount challenges of writing distinct API for different applications. The MOM platform helps to reduce time and associated cost of writing new APIs due to the interoperability capabilities between applications. The summit also consisted of the offers the various issues and constraints in the conception of the OpenMAMA application at its inception in 2004. The most important aspect of this application is the features of publish-subscribe, message queues and the topic based techniques that allows different types of financial bodies to access and use the OpenMAMA.

It is also good to note that without this OpenMAMA software, each application will have to be written to a new API. This will be time consuming and also expensive to build. Hence, the openmama framework remains a viable and acceptable architecture that can help organizations and companies to save cost in terms of the applicability of these concepts.

Further, the absence of this technology is seen to lock organizations down to proprietary solution that are not easy to maintain and customized to suite the features that are desirable. How this application has been leveraged is also very important. This technology allows you to only code your application once. This advantage in this regards is that you do not have to be locked down to a particular vendor. It facilitates the ease of upgrade. The middleware allows the ease of adaptability to fit changing features. Apart from this, the technology is further strengthened by the support for multiple middleware with multiple applications.

Currently, it supports four middleware platforms. In this work, the author will also review these platforms, their functionality and constraints in a perfect way. Another perspective of the OpenMAMA technology is the open solution, which enables anyone to write a middleware bridge to complement the current functionality of the OpenMAMA platforms. It allows the compatibility of third party applications the technology and makes both application and middleware pluggable and interchangeable. Another unique property of this technology is that it provides various added features from the contributors since it is an open source application.

The Importance of OpenMAMA API in financial sector is as follows:
- Allow users to accept new middleware technology and programs as the industry innovates
- Independent from middleware technologies
- Helps companies rate up their time-to-market for event motivated programs and enhance their messaging middleware technology
- High potential for industry transmission outside of the financial sector, towards other areas such as Telecom, High Performance Computing, Web Services and Logistics

There is a new free source API called SMART API creates revolution in the financial APIs market. SMART API has now added a new domain in case of financial engineering. It is most commonly used in for making apps that are used in severe clinical purpose. It has a higher rate of compatibility than others which really makes it even more to be used for.

It has a lightweight medical data model which helps to make it even more useful. The way SMART API is used to make sophisticated Apps and having been allowed in different programming language like Java, Ruby and Python is really great in the financial program developing context.

OpenMAMA & SMART API's can play important role in the financial software design point of view. OpenMAMA & SMART API's API features from software design point of view are as follows:

- OpenMAMA & SMART API's is a free API that provides top rated middleware agnostic messaging API those connections with a variety of concept focused middleware technology.
- OpenMAMA is Licensed under the LGPL 2.1 license so it is verified API for financial software development.
- Hosted at the Linux base in a fairly neutral environment that motivates collaboration.
- These two API's follows free software development methods and processes so anyone can develop new types of financial software by using two API's.
- These two API's support some universal programming languages like C,C++,C#,JNI,JAVA, Python, Rubis on the Rail etc. As a result software developers can easily develop financial software's by using these API's

In summary, this analysis will investigate how the various properties and test of this technology are beneficial to the development of financial engineering API. This analysis will also focus on how the OpenMAMA API platform effect the financial sectors it will also show the necessity of OpenMAMA API in financial engineering. The analysis will be also focusing on how SMART API can contribute on Financial Engineering and why it is considered a low barrier way to design Apps.

Section-C

3.0 Main body of the Analysis

Main body of the analysis is divided into mainly two categories the first have discussed about full detail of the artefact that have written in the first part of the book. In the second category it has answered the general questions. This part has shown the answers of the general questions in detail.

3.1 Full Information of the Artefact of API Based Financial Engineering

During the lifecycle of a transaction many events composite, contingent etc occur. To handle this type of events in a transaction the Financial Transaction Modeling System is needed. It helps to record the payment exchanged with each events with its information. This modeling system will be vastly discussed on this book. Besides, this Financial Transaction Modeling System will be made keeping in mind so that it works both for Smart API and Open MAMA smoothly. A checking will also be conducted on whether programming language like that of Java, JavaScript, C, C++ etc are compatible with this financial model. And finally, in the critical evaluation part of the analysis some example programs related to Open MAMA will be highlighted and discussed. And this example program of Open MAMA which will be discussed is certainly related to the Financial Transaction Modeling System. These are the basic Artifacts of this analysis.

3.2 Constructive API Based Financial Transaction Modeling

The technology and methods are provided to design constructive financial transaction. According to some simple events, branch events, composite events, and/or contingent events associated with a financial transaction are described. The activities may then be used to instantly handle the transaction during the transaction's lifecycle. In one embodiment, at least one easy event associated with a payment exchange is determined, along with an exchange amount and an exchange time frame. At least one division event associated with a set of easy activities is also described, along with a branch date and a branch selector. In addition, at least one blend event associated with a plurality of the easy activities or division activities is determined. The transaction may then be instantly operating during the transaction's lifecycle based at least in part on the simple events, the branch events, and the composite events.

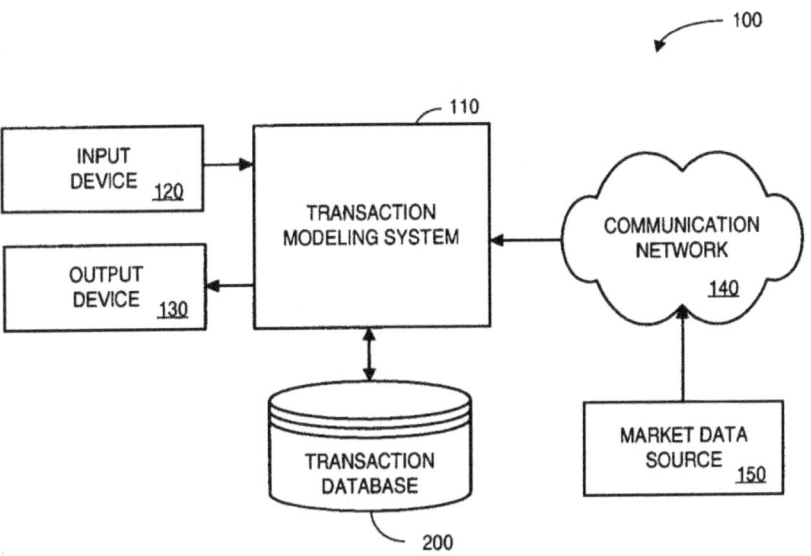

Figure 1: Constructive Financial Transaction Modeling System

3.2.1 Case Study of Constructive API Based Financial Transaction Modeling

A party who confirms to start a transaction may need to determine a number of different circumstances associated with the transaction. For example, the party may want to determine when and how regular payments will be made, the ways in which the amount of various payments will be measured, and/or how various activities will be managed during the transaction's lifecycle (e.g., when the other party want to clarify the transaction). By perfectly interpreting the circumstances of the transaction, various activities can understand and achieve an agreement as to how the transaction will be conducted.

To accomplish the meaning of such a transaction, a system may use a pre-defined type of transaction agreement, such as one associated with the International Swaps and Derivatives Association (ISA) expert agreement or other types of agreement components. In some situations, a financial tool-kit such as the ones available from LEXIFI SAS of Italy may be used to help explain the transaction.

In the same way, the Financial Products Markup Language (FPML), which is an Extensible Markup Terminology (XML) conventional for over-the-counter trading among financial instructions, may be used to implement pre-defined contract terms, parties, and/or payments associated with a transaction.

Different types of transaction, however, will be associated with different types of circumstances. Thus, a new type of transaction might require that a current agreements. Transaction modeling programming language is customized to back up a new type of phrase to be able to completely and perfectly explain the transaction.

By way of example, a new FPML phrase might need to be personally designed to be able to explain a new type of transaction. Consequently, the automated of a transaction meaning system may be restricted (e.g., because a customer needs to personally make a new phrase to explain a new type of transaction).

Moreover, personally developing new circumstances can improve the cost and time required to determine a new transaction—especially when a complicated transaction is being designed. Moreover, problems may happen when a new phrase is designed (e.g., a new phrase might have a random impact under certain conditions) and such problems can be difficult to discover and take care of.

Some embodiments of the existing innovation are associated with transactions and/or agreements between events. As used herein, the conditions transaction and/or agreement may make reference to any agreement between the events. A transaction might be, for example, a lawful agreement interpreting a set of privileges that can be found between the events, such as an ISDA expert agreement associated with financial instruments and/or transaction mediums (e.g., associated with generally, a currency, a product, an power value, a credit, or an equity).

Observe that only one agreement may be associated with more than two events. Also remember that an agreement may or may not be lawfully executed (e.g., an agreement may simply indicate a casual knowing between parties). Moreover, as used herein the phrase "party" can make reference to any enterprise associated with a transaction or agreement. A system may be, for example, a company, a business organization (e.g., a division within a business), or a person.

Transaction & Transaction Modeling System Examples:

Embodiments described herein may be associated with different types of financial transaction. As one example, a contract such as a "swap agreement" might be made and operating according to any of the embodiments described herein. One type of exchange contract is a transaction in which payments will pay set regular quantities of one currency and another payment will pay set regular quantities of another currency. Observe that expenses might be measured on a notional quantity, and the exchange might include preliminary and/or last expenses that match to the notional quantity. Other illustrations of financial transaction might include a loan, a protection, a financial device, or a mixture or insurance contract.

The Transaction Life cycle: In fewer cases embodiments, the Transaction Modeling program "figure 1"show "110" is used to different factors during the lifecycle of a transaction, such as by ageing the transaction. For example, an older transaction model such as easy activities according to some embodiments.

In this situation, believe that the costs time frame symbolizes the present time frame. Events that happened before costs time frame (e.g., which have already been performed) are hidden. That is, those activities have been set and cannot be modified.

Observe that financial operations associated with an easy event might be hidden even though the easy event itself has not been conducted (e.g., when the statement time frame of the financial visible is before time frame of the resource transfer). In this way, the present condition of a financial device can be showed.

Transaction Modeling Management System Example: Observe that a business may need to handle a financial transaction during the transaction's lifecycle. For example, a party might start a transaction that must be monitored with regard to schedules and/or financial market information associated with types and problem control.

Moreover, the status of the transaction may need to be operating (e.g., an agreement might be awaiting or canceled) and the system may need to keep a record of different types of activities associated with the transaction (e.g., a transaction amount may need to be measured and compensated on a regular basis). Monitoring and handling such a transaction can be a moment intensive and costly procedure. The procedure may be even more challenging with regard to transaction that last for a prolonged time period (e.g., a transaction might have a ten year lifecycle).

Moreover, problems might happen (e.g., a transaction might be measured incorrectly) and be challenging to appropriate measurement. Moreover to interpreting financial operations, simple activities, division activities, conditional activities, and/or blend activities. "Figure 1" shows the modeling system "110" might accomplish the use of operating business things to monitor and/or provide transaction operations.

As the induce condition was pleased, the conditional event on that date is conducted. That is, it is determined whether or not the system selects to clarify the transaction. If the system indicates that the transaction should be stopped, the transaction ends (e.g., by coming into a "null" state). If the system does not clarify the transaction, the next blend event will be conducted when the time comes.

According to some embodiments, to assisting costs computations a blend event will not include the entire set of activities that are associated with a single division event or conditional event. Moreover, note that according to one embodiment, the only types of activities that are permitted be described are easy activities, blend activities, and division activities. In the same way, according to another embodiment the only types of activities that are permitted to be described are easy activities, blend activities, and conditional activities.

According to another embodiment, the only types of activities that are permitted to be described are easy activities, blend activities, division activities, and conditional activities. Such techniques might make simpler the transaction modeling system while still enabling all types of transaction to be made.

The various types of activities described herein can provide a versatile way to explain any number of different types of transaction. As a result, the meaning of the activities may be automated which can reduce time, costs, and problems associated with interpreting a new type of transaction.

Transaction Modeling Management Method: In this case study the author has designed a flow chart that can show the financial transaction modeling management method in a detail format. This flow chart is divided into 5 parts. In the first part "1102" that shows a managed business object that can be use for different state. The Second part "1104" of the flow chart show payment receives event notifications. The Third part "1106" of the flow chart discuss about the issue action request to components apps that will be based on event, pre-defined rules like OpenMAMA or SMART API and events. The Fourth part of the flow chart "1108" show the receive action response plan from the internal components apps. The last part of the flow chart "1110" show the transition state of managed business transaction data.

The Transaction Modeling Management Method flow chart is given below:

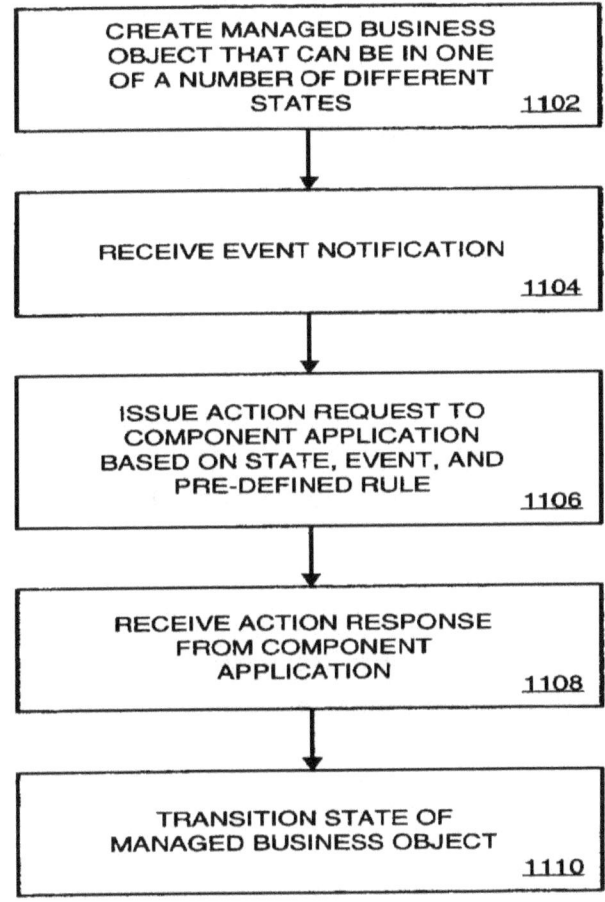

Figure 2: A flow chart of API Based Transaction Modeling Management Method

Now the author has discussed about the flow chart. "Figure 2" is a flow chart of "Transaction Modeling Management Method" for organizations payment transactions are made. For example, information get form a transaction modeling program "110" might be used to create an operating company entity. As another example, a user might review a company procedure and recognize a number of things associated with that procedure (e.g., agreements and cash flows). Moreover, each organizations payment is associated with a plurality of pre-defined conditions (e.g., awaiting and closed). Information about the receiving organizations payment may then be provided to and saved by the transaction management method.

In 1104, event notification is obtained. For example, the transaction management system might get an event notification showing that a voucher transaction is due (e.g., the event notice might be obtained from the transaction modeling program 110 or from an element program).

In1106, an activity demand is released to an element program based on (i) the present a condition of the operating company resource, (ii) the event notice, and/or (iii) a pre-defined concept. The activity demand may be, for example, a demand to the element program asking it to perform some function with regards to an operating resource. For example, the transaction management method might ask an element program to determine the present LIBOR value and re-calculate a transaction quantity associated with an agreement responsibility.

In1108, an activity demand is obtained from the element program (e.g., showing that the activity has been performed). For example, the element program might send an activity demand to the transaction management system showing that a transaction quantity has to be re-calculated (e.g., and the result might be included in the activity demand or the element program might have directly modified a distributed agreement database).

The condition of the receiving organization conditions is changed at 1110 depending on the activity reaction. For example, the transaction management system might convert the condition of receiving organization payment from pending to pay.

In according to some embodiments, handling a transaction includes handling a threat associated with the transaction. For example, a quantity of market threat, interest rate threat, and/or credit rating threat might be measured and used to handle the transaction.

Moreover, handling a transaction system might consist of determining a financial value associated with the transaction. For example, a financial value might be measured centered at least in aspect on the simple activities, the division activities, and the blend activities. The financial value might be associated with, for example, a net existing value, a credit score assessment modification, a lower price value, and/or a cash flow quantity. Methods that might be used to execute the computation consist of S5620 Carlo type models, recursive computations, in reverse introduction, lower price bend costs, Value at Risk (VAR), Credit Value Adjustment (CVA), regular life computations, and/or possibility of exercise principles.

Note that a financial value associated with a transaction might rely at least in aspect on a costs time frame. For example, a net existing value of a transaction measured with regard to one time frame might be different that the net existing value measured with regard to another time frame. Consider a transaction associated with a begin time frame and an end time frame. In this case, the costs time frame might be the present time frame or another irrelevant time frame (e.g., between the begin time frame and the end date). The financial value might then be measured as of, for example, financial visible principles as they persisted or were known on the costs time frame. Moreover, the financial value might be centered at least in aspect on a financially enhanced action or decision.

Transaction Modeling Database System: Transaction modeling database system depends on some APIs like OpenMAMA or SMART API. This systems store lots of transaction history and data in its memory.

The discussion of the above table is given below:

Making reference to "Figure 3", a table symbolizes a transaction data source 200 according to one embodiment of the existing condition. The table contains records that determine one or more transaction and/or relevant principles or activities. The table also describes areas 210, 220, 230 for each of the records. The areas specify: a transaction identifier 210, information 220, and a status 230. The information in the transaction data source 200 may be designed and modified depending on, for example, information obtained from a feedback system 120. According to some embodiments, the customer may offer the information via a Graphical User Interface (GUI).

According to some embodiments, a transaction is designed by interpreting a variety of principles and/or activities in the transaction data source 200. In this situation, the transaction identifier 210 may be, for example, an alphanumeric rule associated with a transaction and a value or event. In the example shown in "Figure 3" the transaction identifier 210 consists of a three types of transaction model concatenated with a three types of value or event model (e.g., the first three records signify activities associated with transaction "T01").

The information 220 describes the associated value or event. For example, the first access is determined as being the London Inter-Bank Provide Rate (LIBOR) value on Jun. 1, 2014. Observe that as used herein, an "event" may make reference to a part of a transaction. For example, the second access is a payment including the transaction of $100 of U.S dollar on Jun. 18, 2014. The status 230 may indicate the status of the value or event (e.g., whether the value or event has been done or is now pending). The image of transaction modeling database system table is given below:

Figure 3: A diagram of the API based transaction modeling database system table

TRANSACTION IDENTIFIER 210	DESCRIPTION 220	STATUS 230
T01_001	LIBOR ON 01JUN06	DONE (1.75)
T01_002	PAY 100 USD ON 18JUN06	PENDING
T01_003	IF T01_001<1.90 THEN T01_002	PENDING
T02_001	LIBOR ON 01JUL06	PENDING
T02_002	PAY 100 USD ON 18JUL06	PENDING
T02_003	IF T02_001<1.90 THEN T02_002	PENDING
T03_001	T01 AND T02	IN PROCESS

Concept Database for Financial Transaction Modeling: Rules of developing a concept database for financial transaction need the help of APIs. For that reason the author has used some coding as an example of concept of transaction database developing. This coding is compatible with SMART & OpenMAMA APIs. Creating referrals to "Figure 4" a table represents the concept databases 1400 that may be used by the control engine 1700 according to an embodiment of the current advancement. The table contains information that figure out one or more recommendations. The table also explains places 1402, 1404, 1406, 1408 for each of the information. The places specify: a Managed Object (MO) type 1402, a concept identifier 1404, a pre-condition 1406, and a post-condition 1408. The facts in the concept databases 1400 may be developed and customized based on APIs, for example, information acquired from the processing system 110 and/or a client.

The operating order type 1402 may be, for example, an alphanumeric concept associated with a type of organization item (e.g., a relationship transaction). The concept identifier 1404 allows several recommendations be described for each operating order type.

1400

MO TYPE 1402	RULE ID 1404	PRE-CONDITION 1406	POST-CONDITION 1408
MO1	M01_R1a	$EVENT_1(MO) + STATE_1$	$COMPONENT_2::ACTION_1(MO)$
MO1	M01_R2	$RESPONSE_1(ACTION_1(MO)) + STATE_1$	$STATE_2$

Figure 4: An Image of API Based Concept Database Table for Financial Transaction Modeling

Each concept is associated with a pre-condition 1406 decoding when the concept is triggered. The pre-condition 1406 may be associated with, for example, getting an event notification (e.g., from the processing system 110), getting an action response, a receiving organization item situation transformation, and/or Boolean features.

The post-condition 1408 explains what should happen when the precondition is satisfied. The post-condition 1408 might be associated with, for example, moving a receiving organization item situation and/or offering an action requirement. Most of the situations, a concept is associated with an invoice of a payment notification. For example, if the operating engine gets an event notification of type "Event" referencing a managed object of type MO when operating order is in state, the management engine might problem an activity demand of type "Action" to element "Components" referencing that operating item. This concept might be described as:

Event(MO)+Statei(MO)→Componentx::Action(MO)

The controlling engine might convert operating order to Statej:

Event(MO)+Statei(MO)→Statej(MO)

According to some embodiments, payments can referrals one, and only one, operating item. In other situations, a concept is associated with an invoice of an activity demand from an element program. For example, if the transaction management engine gets an activity demand of type "Response" referencing an activity demand of type "Action" on an operating order of type MO from Components, when the operating order is in Statei, the transaction management engine1700 might convert the operating order to Statej:

Response(Action(MO))+Statei(MO)→Statej(MO)

Note that an activity demand might be scoped by operating order types, 1. The present condition and 2. The activity demand types. Moreover, in some embodiments, only one activity demand is permitted to be waiting for each operating order (e.g., and thus there is no need to recognize the replying component). In still other situations, when the operating engine changes an operating order of type MO to a particular State, an activity demand of type Action is released to Components referencing the operating object:

$State_z(MO) \rightarrow Component_x::Action(MO)$

State that such a concept can be "path-independent" (e.g., activity demand is show the operation of new condition, not of how the new condition was reached).

Financial Transaction Modeling Operating and Control Engine Example:

Financial transaction modeling needs some operating and control engine for controlling transaction, transaction history and database.
For this purpose it depends on APIs like SMART, Open MAMA or some other APIs. In this example part of financial transaction modeling operating and control engine the author has used some programming coding which are compatible with OpenMAMA and SMART APIs.

The flowchart of Financial Transaction Modeling Operating and Control Engine is given below:

Figure 5: An Image of Financial API Based Transaction Modeling Operating and Control Engine

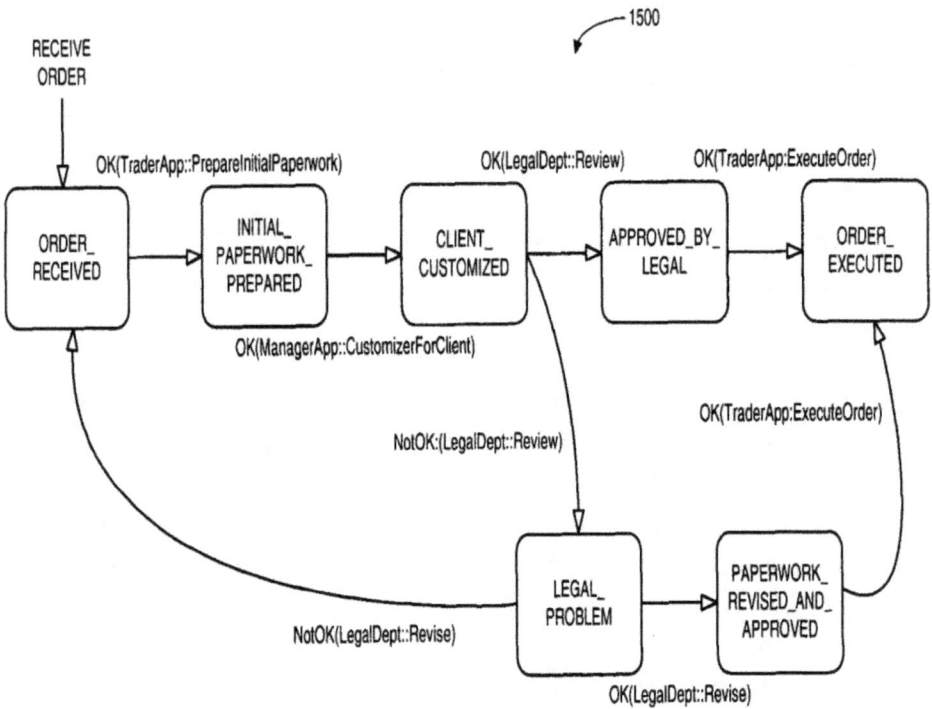

"Figure 5" is an example 1500 of condition transitions according to one embodiment of the existing system. In particular, when a "Receive Order" event notice happens, the following concept causes the transaction management engine to set up an example of a receiver organizations payment and status that example in condition

"ORDER_RECEIVED"
Receive Order→ORDER_RECEIVED

The following concept indicates that when the condition ORDER_RECEIVED is joined, an activity demand is passed on to a "TraderApp" element asking the element to get ready a preliminary set of paperwork:

ORDER_RECEIVED→TraderApp::PrepareInitialPaperwork( )

When the TraderApp element gets this activity demand, it might instantly produce and provide an agreement such as pre-defined get in touch with conditions. When the TraderApp element finishes this process, it sends the following activity demand to the transaction management engine: OK(TraderApp::PrepareInitialPaperwork). Another concept describes that when they receiver organizations payment is in condition RECEIVED_ORDER and an

OK(TraderApp::PrepareInitialPaperwork) is obtained, the transaction management engine will convert that item to condition

INITIAL_PAPERWORK_RECEIVED:
OK(TraderApp::PrepareInitialPaperwork)+ORDER_RECEIVED→
INITIAL_PAPERWORK_RECEIVED

Similarly, the operating & control engine requests a ManagerApp element to change the agreement for the consumer and changes the receiving organization payment to condition CLIENT_CUSTOMIZED after the ManagerApp sends an activity demand showing that the process is finish.

The operating & control engine then requests a LegalDept element to evaluation the agreement (e.g., to figure out that the agreement satisfies regulating specifications. In this situation, however, two guidelines might apply:

OK(LegalDept::Review)+CLIENT_CUSTOMIZED→APPROVED _BY_LEGAL

NotOK(LegalDept::Review)+CLIENT_CUSTOMIZED→LEGAL_ PROBLEM

That is, the LegalDept may react by showing that the processing is finished (and the agreement is approved), in that situation operating & control engine changes the receiving organizations payment to condition APPROVED_BY_LEGAL. The LegalDept can also react by showing that the agreement is not accepted (i.e., NotOK).
In this situation, the management engine changes the receiving organization payment to condition LEGAL_PROBLEM. If the agreement is accepted by the LegalDept program (or if it improved and approved), the transaction is implemented.

The second flowchart of Financial Transaction Modeling Operating and Control Engine is given below:

"Figure 6" demonstrates additional condition changes according to an embodiment of the present innovation. In particular, when a "Cancel Order" event notice is obtained by the management engine 1700, the transaction may or may not be stopped based on the current condition of the receiving organization payment.

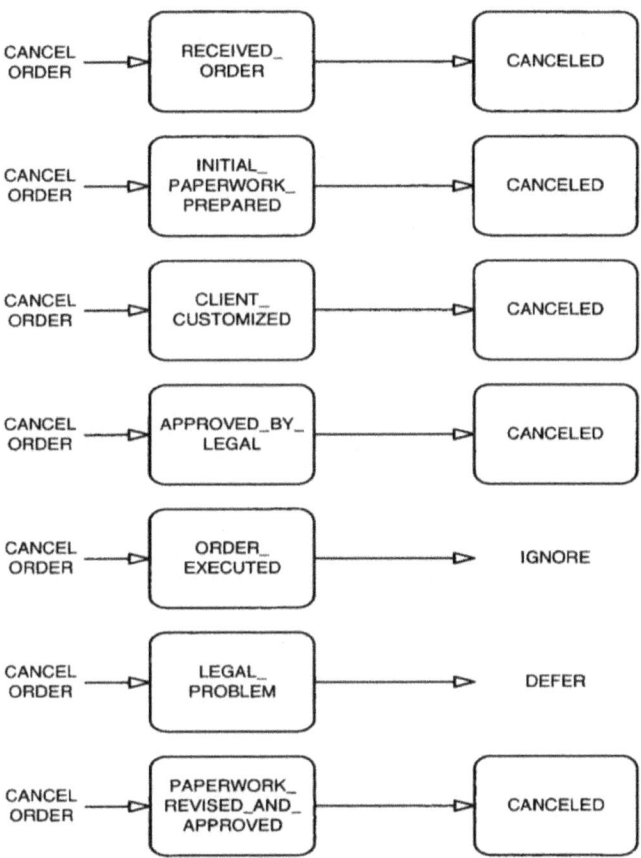

Figure 6: An Image of the API Based Financial Transaction Modeling Operating and Control Engine

For example, if receiving organization payment is in condition INITIAL_PAPERWORK_PREPARED, the transaction management engine 1700 convert receiving organization payment to condition CANCELED. In other cases, however, the transaction management engine 1700 will not respect the Clarify Purchase event notice (e.g. the event notice might be ignored or a decision might be deferred).

Financial Transaction Modeling Operating & Control Engine Apparatus:

This is the most important transaction modeling system. In this part the author has design the financial transaction modeling operating & control engine apparatus. This apparatus engine is based on APIs. So we can use OpenMAMA or SAMRT API in this apparatus engine. The flow chart of financial transaction modeling operating & control engine apparatus is as follows:

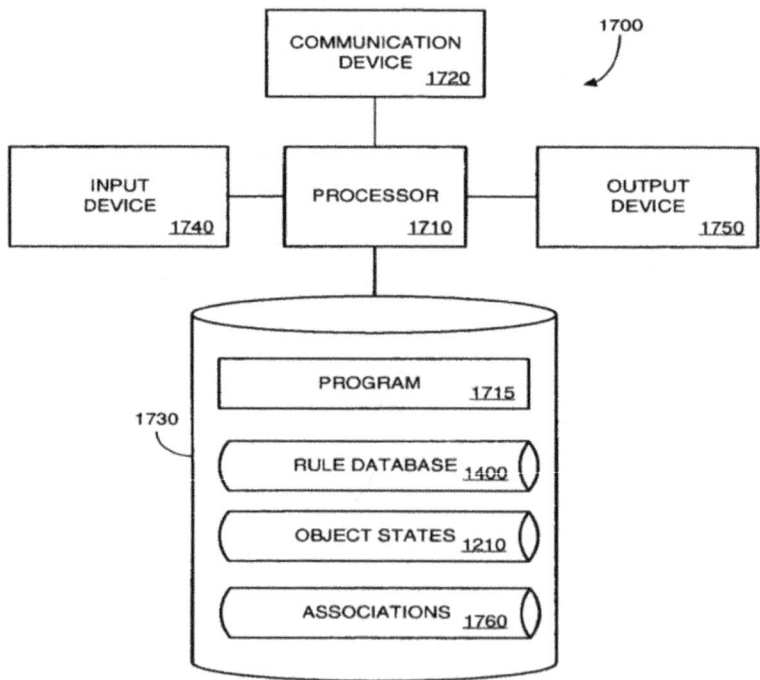

Figure 7: A flow chart of f API based transaction modeling operating & control engine

"Figure 7" is a flow chart of a transaction management operating & control engine 1700 according to some embodiments. The management operating & control engine 1700 includes a processor chip 1710, such as one core or many cores AMD or INTEL processors chip, coupled to an interaction system 1720 designed to connect via an interaction network (not proven in Figure 17). The interaction system 1720 may be used to connect, for example, with one or more transaction modeling systems 110 and/or element system devices. Note that the management engine 1700 may exchange and/or process information, for example, associated with SMART API or other APIs, OpenMAMA or other middleware, a data source, an Application Protocol Interface (API), and/or a SMS or message format.

An input system 1740 (e.g. a mouse or keyboard) may be used to provide information to the transaction management engine 1700 (e.g., so that a concept can be defined). An output system 1750 (e.g., a display system or printer) may be used to receive information from the management operating & control engine 1700.

The processor 1710 is also in interaction with a hard drive 1730. The hard drive 1730 may comprise any appropriate information hard drive, including combinations of modern storage devices (e.g., CD, DVD, Floppy Disk, Pen Drive and Hard Disk), optical or Blu-Ray storage devices, and/or semiconductor storage devices such as Random Access Memory (RAM) devices and Read Only Memory (ROM) devices.

The hard drive 1730 use a system 1715 for controlling the processor 1710. The processor 1710 performs instructions of the system 1715. For example, the processor 1710 may manage organization payment state transitions in accordance with any of the embodiments described herein.

As used herein, information may be "received" by or "transmitted" to, for example: (i) the transaction management engine 1700 from an element application; or (ii) an application or element within the transaction management engine 1700 from another application, element, or any other source.

As proven in "Figure 17", the hard drive 1730 also use a concept data source 1400 and item declares 1210. According to some embodiments, the hard drive further organizations 1760. For example, the transaction management engine 1700 might associate receiving organization payment with one or more other receiving organization payments. Consider agreement of organization payment that is associated with 30 cash flow statement. In this way, an event notice associated with the agreement of organizations payment might instantly convert declare of the 30 cash flow statement task (e.g., when the agreement is stopped all of the cash flows could be instantly canceled).

Element Program: It's a unique component of financial transaction modeling. For this task the author has used APIs as element program or component application. The graphical diagram of this element program component is as follows:

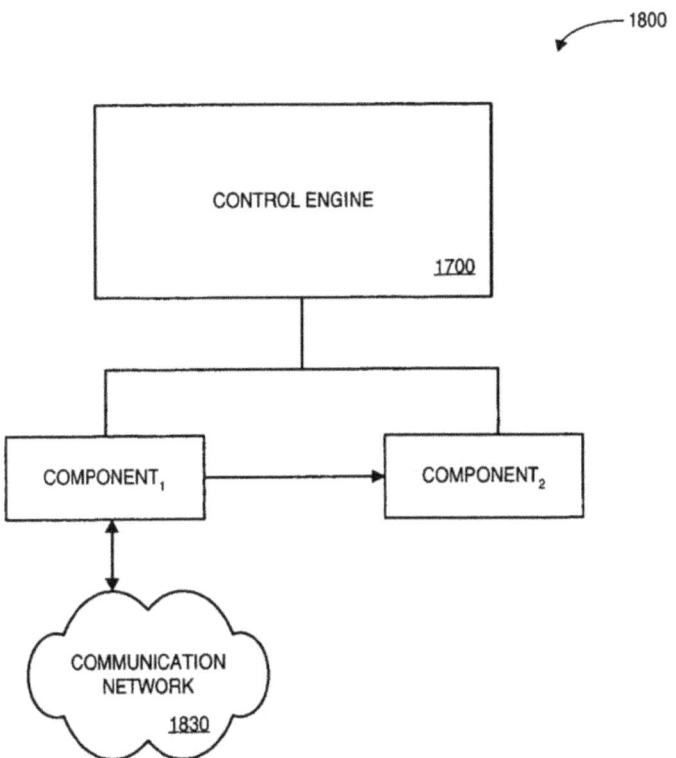

Figure 8: A Graphical Diagram of the Element Program Component

"Figure 8" is an element program summary of a system 1800 according to another embodiment of the existing system. As before, the transaction management engine 1700 is collected transactions information by using a program element. Observe that one element might not even be conscious of the transaction lifecycle of another element (although it may be conscious of the transaction management engine1700, which will understand of the other component). Moreover, a current program might not need significant variations in order to interface with the management engine 1700.

In accordance with some embodiments, Component1 can also transfers information straight to Component 2. For example, the management engine 1700 might deliver an activity demand to Component1 asking that a transaction amount be re-calculated in accordance with the existing LIBOR amount.

In this case, Component1 accesses the existing LIBOR amount via an interaction system 1830. Moreover, Component1 sends the existing LIBOR amount straight to Component 2 (which needs the information to react to an upcoming activity demand that will be produced by the transaction management engine 1700).

One benefits of such a strategy is that the information does not need to passed on from Component1 to the transaction management engine 1700 and then again from the management engine 1700 to Component 2. Moreover, Component 2 might be able to start controlling the information even before getting an activity demand from the management engine 1700.

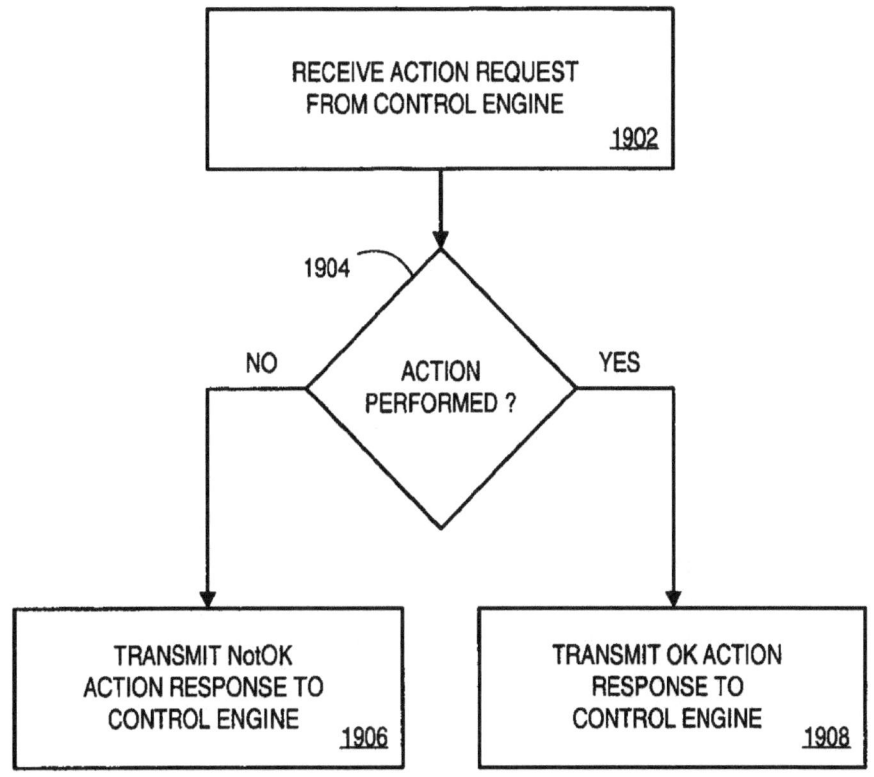

Figure 9: A Diagram of Element Program Method for API Based Transaction Modeling

"Figure 9" is a flow chart diagram of an element program method according to some embodiments. At 1902, an activity demand is obtained from a operating and control engine 1700. The activity demand might, for example, ask the element program to execute order, such as operate that content an event notice or carries out an activity relevant to an operating order (e.g., to produce a review using a template).

As the activity is not conducted at 1904, a NotOK activity demand is passed on to the operating and control engine 1700 at 1906. For example, an element program might not be able to execute an activity because of a government control. If the activity is conducted at 1904, an OK activity demand is passed on to the control engine 1700 at 1908. According to some embodiments, a program may continually execute activities (e.g., the program may follow a concept or produce an exemption when there is no appropriate rule).

Thus, some embodiments may effectively control the organized things. Moreover, the control program and relevant resources may provide assured, rule-based, effectively requested, reliable performance of features by a set of separate elements and the concomitant control of the declares of a set of organized things, in reaction to possibly competitive asynchronous activities. In addition, the program is scalable (e.g., a huge number of organized things may be managed) and the granularity of the things and guidelines may be chosen as appropriate.

Transaction Modeling Graphical User Interface (GUI) System:

This last part of financial modeling .In this part the Graphical User Interface (GUI) system show transaction modeling result via computer monitor display system or other devices display system such as Laptop, Smart Phone, Tablet PC, TAB etc. For this purpose the transaction modeling system use APIs interface program and coding. The author has shown SMART and OpenMAMA APIs compatible coding for this task. The diagram of Transaction Modeling Graphical User Interface (GUI) System is given below:

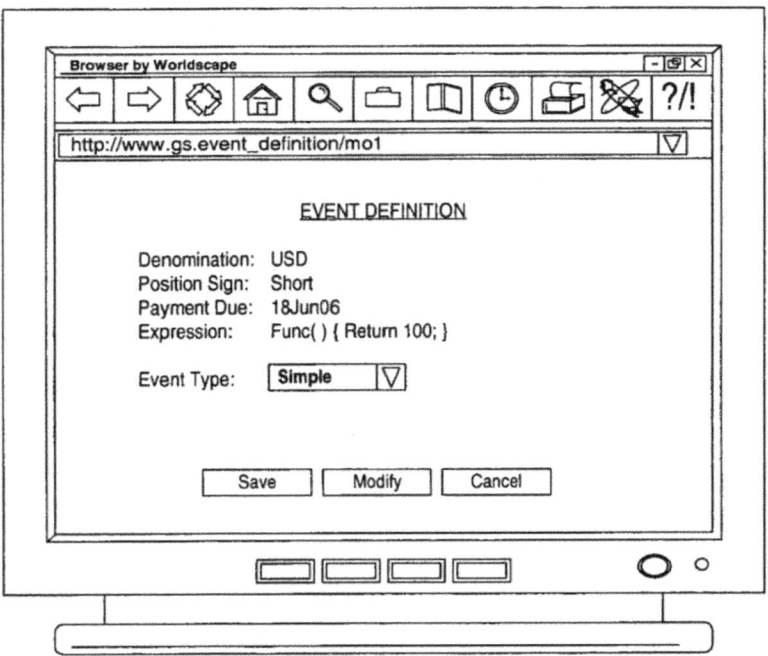

Figure 10: A Diagram of API Based Transaction Modeling Graphical User Interface (GUI) System

"Figure 10" diagram show in 2000 (e.g., laptop, tablet computer monitor or other smart devices display) in accordance with one embodiment of the existing system. In particular, the diagram 2000 provides a user interface to accomplish the meaning of activities, such as simple activities, conditional activities, division activities, blend activities, and/or financial operations. The customer may also choose to "Save" the event or financial visible, to "Modify" event or financial visible, and/or to "Cancel" the function.

3.3 Recommendations for Constructive API Based Financial Transaction Modeling

Now a day's financial transaction modeling system is very much popular in the financial sectors. Constructive financial transaction is necessary for any types of financial organizations. A constructive financial transaction process can organize and secure the financial transaction process. API based system can develop constructive financial transaction process.

So making good constructive transaction modeling system is necessary for any types of financial organization. API based transaction modeling is much reliable then analog or normal programming based transaction modeling system. So the analysis has tried hard to develop a best and secure transaction modeling system for financial organization. In this book the author has developed a Constructive Financial Transaction Modeling System. This system is mainly API based transaction modeling system and it uses the constructive financial transaction process.

Although some illustrations have been described with regard to particular types of transaction process, embodiments may be used with other types of transaction, such as exchange payment associated with fast straddle and/or a continuous payment exchange. Moreover, some embodiments have been described here in with regard to particular types of company transaction, but the existing system may be used in any other type of organizations payment transaction purposes. Moreover, the particular financial operations, activities, and guidelines offer herein are merely for representation and embodiments may be associated with other types of information the existing system has been described with regards to several embodiments completely for the objective of representation.

Individual experienced in the financial engineering will identify from this information that the innovation is not restricted to the embodiments described, but may be used with variations restricted only by the opportunity of the transaction statements. This analysis has recommended some APIs for develop this financial modeling system.

3.4 Summary of the Constructive API Based Financial Transaction Modeling Analysis

This analysis develops an API based financial transaction modeling system for constructive financial transaction. In one embodiment of the present innovation, at least one easy event associated with a payment exchange is determined, along with an exchange quantity and an exchange time. At least one division event associated with a set of easy activities is also described, along with a division time frame and a division selector. In addition, at least one blend event associated with a plurality of the easy activities or division activities is determined. The transaction may then be instantly managed during the transaction's lifecycle based at least in aspect on the easy activities, the division activities, and the blend activities. The existing innovation presents a financial transaction modeling system.

This innovation is necessary for any type of financial organization like bank, insurance company, hospital, leasing company etc. In the modern time most of the programming interface is based on APIs so this OpenMAMA, SMART APIs based financial transaction modeling system is helpful for all types of business and financial organization. Because it is the most secure and fast financial transaction modeling system in the world of financial engineering.

3.5 Answering the General Question

In the "general question" part of the analysis has shown 4 general questions about API based financial engineering. The questions are very much useful and important for the research. The general questions of this book were as follows:

1. Investigate and review financial transaction models using APIs based on OpenMAMA in real-life scenarios.

2. Research the use of OpenMAMA in the present financial sectors.

3. Research on Smart API and how can it help in the sectors of financial engineering.

4. Research the proper use of OpenMAMA in financial modeling.

The analysis has already discussed about no. 1 and no.4 question answers in the artefact part. These two questions are based on financial transaction modeling and researching the proper use of OpenMAMA in financial modeling. The analysis has totally discussed about these two questions in the artefact part. It has also provided case study based research result, detail recommendations and summery of the research.

Now it has discussed about the answers of no.2 and no.3 questions. These two questions are closely related to each other. Because these question are based on open source APIs. The question no. 2 is based on researching about OpenMAMA API in the present financial sectors and the question no. 3 is based on researching about Smart API and how can it help in the sectors of financial engineering.

The answers of general questions no.2 and no.3 are given below:

3.5.1 The Use of OpenMAMA in the Present Financial Sectors

The author has discussed detail information of OpenMAMA in this part of the book. Before discussing about the use of OpenMAMA in the present financial sectors the detail discussion is given below:

The MAMA (Middleware Agnostic Messaging) API is a registration centered messaging API with publish/subscribe semantics, which provides a light and portable abstraction on top of a wide range of actual messaging middlewares. The OpenMAMA API provides programmers with a typical interface to the actual messaging API, enabling migration from one messaging API to another without any rule changes to programs designed using the API. The API provides an asynchronous, event-driven development structure. The organizations use the API to provide callbacks where needed. Information is spread returning to the authorized program via these callbacks in reaction to distributing of activities from connection lines. Industry data semantics are included through the use of the OpenMAMDA API.

The OpenMAMA API also provides specs when used on the NYSE Technologies Market Data Infrastructure such as:
- Registration transaction using secure network
- Right enforcement for better financial task messaging.
- Initial values/recaps for financial transaction modeling.
- Information & Data quality
- Renew messages
- Team subscriptions

There are mainly two operating systems which are currently supported to OpenMAMA API:

- Linux
- Windows

There are some middlewares which are currently supported to OpenMAMA API platform:
- Avis

- NYSE Technologies Data Fabric (as an individual connect in for Information Material clients only).

- 29West LBM (as a personal link in for Information Content customers only).

- Some popular programming languages are used for the OpenMAMA API reveal the same top stage things with the same development interface. Unless specified, allowance of OpenMAMA objects and development of OpenMAMA things are two individual actions.

The first thing allocates the storage and the second initializes the item. Each of the API implementations is line secure and line conscious. All functions/methods in the API, across all terminology implementations and carries, display the same behavior, unless otherwise mentioned.

The supported programming languages names are given below:
- C
- C++
- C#
- JNI

OpenMama uses a typical publish/subscribe idiom (pub/sub). In this messaging design the information are not sent straight to the devices, but released to a subject. Members show attention in one or more subjects, and get only information that attention them. This decoupling of marketers and subscribers allows for higher scalability.

The features and advantages of OpenMAMA are given below:
- OpenMAMA is a free program that provides a top rated middleware agnostic messaging API that connections with a variety of concept focused middleware systems.
- Licensed under the LGPL 2.1 license.
- Hosted at the Linux base in a fairly neutral environment that motivates collaboration.
- Follows free development methods and processes.
- Includes start and available e-mail information, resource rule database, and bug monitoring systems.
- Participation is start to any designer, organization or enterprise, provided that they stick to the terms of the book, and the LGPL 2.1.
- It allows programmers to develop programs for market more easily and quickly, within any industry-standard middleware atmosphere, regardless of the system facilities.
- It guarantees top rated both with regards to throughput and concept latency.
- It provides common function at API level but independence to distinguish both at reduced and greater loads (example: middleware technological innovation and applications).

OpenMAMA API in the Present Financial Sectors: Now the analysis is discussing about the use of OpenMAMA in the present financial sectors. The discussion is as follows:

The free source application has been at the center of recent banking organizations and investment marketplaces for several years. Free source API design for creating application is now also taking main part in the financial sectors. OpenMAMA is an attempt to develop a source execution of the MAMA (Middleware Agnostic Messaging API) that financial services organizations use for moving information across messaging programs. OpenMAMA was first declared this year.

The OpenMAMA book contains big titles in the financial services industry such as financial institution of the United States, Bank of America, Merrill Lynch, J.P. Morgan and NYSE Technologies. Financial engineering can track its connection with open source technology back to when companies started implementing PC-based web servers with x86 chipsets across the business. This was the initial trend of consumer of IT, as pc structure forced server design.
Although previously open source tasks focused on typical business needs (operating techniques, web servers and middleware), the financial solutions market released a number of its own industry specific tasks such as the Open Middleware Agnostic Messaging API (OpenMAMA), Complex Event Processing (CEP) Engine Esper, and FIX messaging entrance, QuickFIX tasks to make use of the advantages of open source development.

The typical line among these tasks is that they were created from a technological need and stimulated by a few technologists who identified the value in open cooperation. For example, OpenMAMA serves companies like Bank of America, Merrill Lynch, J.P. Morgan and NYSE Technologies a typical abstraction part for several messaging techniques.

Back in the 90's, there might have been aggressive benefits between concept techniques, but they have since grown up to a factor where they are almost interchangeable.

By implementing OpenMAMA in such a different financial environment, standard banking software programmers only need to learn one free API instead of hanging out perfecting multiple APIs, which saves organizations efforts and money. According to the research result of NYSE Technologies, the Business Version of OpenMAMA is an examined and qualified submission of OpenMAMA and provides an open, vendor-neutral incorporation part for middleware messaging. At NYSE Technology, OpenMAMA has become a primary part of its Open System effort. OpenMAMA significantly decreases the rubbing and complexness between other internal designed or exterior technology, when developing or switching from one to another, at both the middleware and program layer.

3.5.2 Research on Smart API and how can it Help in the Sectors of Financial Engineering

SMART API is a new open source API developed by SMART Organization. SMART Organization is a non-profitable organization just like Linux. This API is mainly based on medial engineering and health apps developing programming interface. As it is a new API still it is mainly used in medical and health apps developing task. SMART API is a features of a free system based on web features for building substitutable applications on health care information techniques such as electronic recovery information, personal recovery information, medical information system and wellness information transactions. The SMART API features are designed to help fix the problems in both revealing healthcare information to applications and the creation of innovative substitutable applications for these techniques.

There are some programming languages which are much compatible with this new API platform. The names of these programming languages are as follows:
- C
- C++
- C#
- JNI
- Java Spring
- Ruby on Rails
- Python/Django

The 3 Primary Elements of the SMART API Architecture Design are given below:

The first part of the SMART galaxy is the environment of SMART programs created by programmers desperate to bring solutions in the hands of physicians and patients. For example, these programs can be drugs supervisors, diabetic issues assessment supervisors, or lab results visualizes. These programs can be allocated via a future app store.

Next it has the servers which are the information suppliers in the SMART galaxy. The server could be personally managed wellness information techniques, electronic medical information techniques, wellness information transactions, or other suppliers. Regardless of type, a package is accountable for revealing the SMART API to the programs and providing a perspective in which the programs run.

Lastly, it has the interface which allows the programs and server to connect to each other using the SMART application development interface (API). The API is what keeps the programs and the server decoupled from each other enabling the users to mix and match them.

Also, the API allows the substitutability of the SMART programs. From the viewpoint of an app the server are substitutable, because they all reveal the same interface and the app can run on any one of them. In the same way from the viewpoint of the package, the programs are substitutable. The package manager is totally able to pick the programs that he/she needs. And if an app better suited to his/her needs comes along, he/she can substitute the current app with the new one.

In order to keep things simple, an app operates against one package at a time. The package, however, is totally able to get connected to several information resources and total information as needed.

The SMART system describes four main components:

SMART API is a developer-friendly information model protecting the most widely used medical information elements such as problems, medicines, laboratories, vital signs, activities, and fulfillments. The information is meaningfully organized with sources to appropriate programming systems and appropriate information is connected. For example, a given satisfaction sources the appropriate medication which sources a specific RxNorm rule.

- An easy to use REST API to access the information designs above

- Simple set of features based on widely used, off-the-shelf methods for app signing up, authentication, and authorization

- Set of software development tools and certification such as local customer collections for JavaScript, Python, iOS, and Coffee (the SMART Framework) and a Referrals EMR for examining generally known as the "SMART Referrals Container".

The author has done some research about this new platform of open source API. The research and analysis has found various types of information about this API. So, these API is mostly compatible with the medical engineering task and less compatible with financial apps making purposes. Because it has limitation in its original programming codes which are specially made for medical engineering purposes.

But in this research the author wants to show this API is useful for financial task. Because the analysis has seen that now a day's some financial organizations use this API in their daily financial services as well. In the artefact part the analysis has discussed the use of this API in the development of financial modeling. It has also written some useful coding which related to financial modeling services based on SMART API. So, the author hopes in future SMART API will be more useful like OpenMAMA in the world of financial engineering.

Section-D

4.0 Conclusion

In this section, the analysis has discussed about the successfulness of this book. The discussion is given below:

Financial Engineering is subject which is important for all types of financial institutions. Now days financial engineering is depended on APIs based system which is more reliable and less time consume for financial task. In this task a new API called OpenMAMA conquer the markets. Besides medical engineering based API called SMART API also has done well in financial engineering task.

Traditionally, the various applications and technologies alternative provide financial organization a very fragmented service. As the world changes into the digital age, though, this scenery is fast changing. Due to the availability introduced about by having near-universal availability "the cloud" from any computer or device and any location. And the appearance of Application Development Interfaces (APIs) that allow different application programs to incorporate in a way that has never before been possible.

These changes in turn are driving several new growing applications design. The first is that now independent application companies are often bigger and better developed than exclusive alternatives, which both encourages in new companies to innovate and also makes it much easier than ever for consultants to modify companies knowing that they will have more convenient customer and company information and availability similar (or even better) application after making a development.

As of now, these developments are still ongoing and will be playing out for many years. However, the track is clear and extremely positive for both start-up companies who have more opportunity for development and success than ever and also consultants, who may enjoy application in the future that is at the same time less expensive, more efficient, more impressive, more incorporated, and just absolutely excellent to anything we've ever had in the past.

The first is the rise of the internet and an ever growing amount of data transfer usages has made it possible to link with program mainly through electronic connection. Program no more needs to run on your pc in order for you to use it. Instead, it can be available "in the cloud" and still be utilized from your pc. Although the near phrase benefit is simply that companies no more have to buy their own components to run local set -ups of program, the long run effect is far more profound with cloud-based processing, your program can be utilized from any location, and any device which also means it can be utilized from any company and on any advisory system.

The second significant pattern has been the appearance of Application Development Interfaces (APIs). The basic concept of an API is that program is designed with various hook varieties and opportunities, which allow developers from other companies to program their program to link with, attach on to, and link with the first program.

The aims of the book were as follows:

1. Investigate and review financial transaction models using APIs based on OpenMAMA in real-life scenarios.

2. Research the use of OpenMAMA in the present financial sectors.

3. Research on Smart API and how can it help in the sectors of financial engineering.

4. Research the proper use of OpenMAMA in financial modeling.

The book has tried hard to discuss about its all aims in this analysis.

The objectives of the book were as follows:
- The capability to calculate, store, process, use and re-use information of all types' transaction and from all resources easily and to make it available anywhere from several devices.

- Computerized low-maintenance techniques that allow for easy replication.

- The capability to considerably generate down handling costs.

- New techniques to creating firmly incorporated techniques based on best-of-class components.

- Improved performance and removing errors form the system.

- Developing financial software by using OpenMAMA API in C/C++ programming language.

- Find the advantages and disadvantages of OpenMAMA API.

- Researching the best features of OpenMAMA API for financial engineering.

- Research on features and advantages of Smart API.

- To analyze how Smart API can help in different sectors of financial engineering.

The analysis has tried to fulfill its all objectives and aims in that book. The author develops a financial modeling system and constructive transaction process. He also develops API based financial modeling system. This analysis also has discussed about SMART and OpenMAMA API's. This analysis is also investigated OpenMAMA example programs and discusses their uses in the critical evaluation part. The author is fulfilled his all types of research works in this book. So this book is helpful for the future API based financial engineering research works.

Section-E

5.0 Critical evaluation

Critical evaluation is a very important section of an analysis. The author has developed a resource full critical evaluation in this part. In this part the book has investigate some example program of OpeMAMA. These example programs are necessary for API based financial engineering and middleware agnostic financial messaging.

The investigated OpenMAMA example programs and their descriptions are as follows:

Example Program	Description
MamaListen	This is a simple *OpenMAMA* application that creates a configurable number of subscriptions to a single source on a single transport. Received messages for these subscriptions are printed to screen with name, fid, type, and value. This application shows the basic operation of a market data application.
MamaPublisher	This is a simple publishing application that uses basic publishing to send messages with a few fields on a well-known topic. Its purpose is to show the use of basic publishing for non-market data.
MamaSubscriber	This application uses basic subscriptions to listen for a basic publisher. It works in conjunction with MamaPublisher. This application shows the other side of non-market data communication.
MamaInbox	This application sends an inbox request to a source and waits for a reply. When used in conjunction with MamaPublisher, the MamaPublisher will listen for the request and respond with a simple message. This illustrates the request/reply mechanism as used with both market data and non-market data situations.
MamaIO	This application shows how to use *OpenMAMA* to monitor a file descriptor for input.
MamaMultiSubscriber	This application demonstrates how to use multiple bridges within a single application to receive data from two middlewares. The received messages are processed and displayed in the same manner.
MamaProxy	This application is similar to MamaListenCached, with the added functionality that the messages are republished using the market data publishing component (DQPublisher). This allows a further MamaListen client to receive the data via this path, rather than directly from the source.
MamaSymbolListSubscriber	This application uses a symbol list subscription to get a complete list of all symbols available from the source, and then makes market data subscriptions to these symbols, illustrating how to listen to the "world" in topic terms.
MamaFtMember	This application demonstrates use of *OpenMAMA* fault tolerance capability. Each instance of MamaFtMember can be assigned to a group. Each instance within the group has a fault tolerance weight. Whenever all members in a group are active, the highest weighted member will report its status as ACTIVE, the others will be STANDBY. If the highest weighted member is killed the next highest weighted member will become ACTIVE.

Section-F

References and Bibliography

Robert Dubil. (2011). *Financial Engineering and Arbitrage in the Financial Markets Wiley.*

Markus Reitz and Ulrich N' ogel. (2006). Components: A valuable investment for Financial Engineering. *Why derivative contracts should be Active Documents, Proceedings of the 4th International symposium on Principles and practice of programming in Java.*

Darryl K. Taft. (2012). *OpenMAMA: Book Delivers First Release of Middleware Messaging API.*

WHITE PAPER. (2012). *OpenMAMA: Open source messaging API for the capital markets, NYSE Technologies.*

Feargal O' Sullivan .(2012). *OpenMAMA: open middleware standards for the capital Markets and beyond. Full Linux Collaboration Summit .*[online] available from <http://www.youtube.com/watch?v=UTPkXu_lTa8>[10th Dec 2013]

The Linux Foundation. (2012). *Introduction to OpenMAMA.*[online] available from <http://www.openmama.org/what-is-openmama/introduction-to-openmama> [10th Dec 2013]

The SMART API Organization. (2014). *About SMART API.*[online] available from <http://smartplatforms.org/for-developers/> [15th MAR 2014]

The SMART API Organization. (2014). *How SMART API works.* [online] available from <http://docs.smartplatforms.org/guide/>[21th MAR 2014]

About the Author

Ghazi Mokammel Hossain is a professional e-book, article, research paper, analysis and creative writer. He has written many articles, research papers, analysis and creative articles. He is also a freelance writer & researcher. The author lives in Dhaka, Bangladesh. He was born in 31 December 1993. The name of his father is Ghazi Mozammel Hossain and his mother name is Syeda Taskin Ara. He has passed his S.S.C exam from Narinda Govt. High School, Dhaka under Dhaka Board in 2008 and passed his H.S.C exam from Ideal Commerce College, Dhaka under Dhaka Board in 2010. Now he is studying in BBA (Honors) 4th year in Victoria University Bangladesh. He has also completed Computer Science and Engineering certificate course in 2011.He has published his first book called "IPv4 IP6 Technology & Implementation" in Amazon kindle and Createspace.com on 2013. And he has published his second book called "Introduction to Network on Chip Routing Algorithms" on 2014. Playing football, Cricket, PC games, Reading book, research paper, cycling and mountain climbing are his favorite hobbies.

www.ingramcontent.com/pod-product-compliance
Lightning Source LLC
Chambersburg PA
CBHW071811170526
45167CB00003B/1262

Detail Information of the Book:

Authored by: Ghazi Mokammel Hossain

Editing and Proofread by: i. Syed Shaheer Uddin Ahmed
ii. Jhon Albert

Preface by: Mohammed Fathe Mubin

Designed by: Ghazi Mokammel Hossain

Publications Format: Amazon Kindle E-Book format, Amazon Createspace Paper back format

Edition No: First Edition

Publication From: Dhaka, Bangladesh

Version: International Version

Published by: GM Publishers, associated with Amazon Kindle Direct Publishing & Createspace

ISBN:

ISBN-13: 978-1502802354

ISBN-10: 150280235X (The book has been assigned a CreateSpace ISBN)

Contact Address:
Email address: gmjon21@gmail.com
Skype Id: gmhossain380
Phone no: +8801674950802